CHARLES DICKENS'S A CHRISTMAS CAROL

AN AQA ESSAY WRITING GUIDE

R. P. DAVIS

For Rosaline.

CONTENTS

FOREWORD

In your GCSE English Literature exam, you will be presented with an extract from Charles Dickens's *A Christmas Carol* and a question that asks you to offer both a close analysis of the extract plus a commentary of the novella as a whole. Of course, there are many methods one *might* use to tackle this style of question. However, there is one particular technique which, due to its sophistication, most readily allows students to unlock the highest marks: namely, **the thematic method**.

To be clear, this study guide is *not* intended to walk you through the novella scene-by-scene: there are many great guides out there that do just that. No, this guide, by sifting through a series of mock exam questions, will demonstrate *how* to organise a response thematically and thus write a stellar essay: a skill we believe no other study guide adequately covers!

I have encountered students who have structured their essays all sorts of ways: some by writing about the extract line by line, others by identifying various language techniques and giving each its own paragraph. The method I'm advocating, on the other hand, involves picking out three to four themes that will allow you to holistically answer the question: these three to four themes will become the three to four content paragraphs of your essay, cushioned between a brief introduction and conclusion. Ideally, these themes will follow from one to the next to create a flowing argument. Within each of these thematic paragraphs, you can then ensure you are jumping through the mark scheme's hoops.

So to break things down further, each thematic paragraph will include various point-scoring components. In each paragraph, you will quote from the extract, offer analyses of these quotes, then discuss how the specific language techniques you have identified illustrate the theme you're discussing. In each paragraph, you will also discuss how other parts of the novella further illustrate the theme (or even complicate it). And in each, you will comment on the era in which the novella was written and how that helps to understand the chosen theme.

Don't worry if this all feels daunting. Throughout this guide, I will be illustrating in great detail – by means of examples – how to build an essay of this kind.

Charles Dickens.

The Dickensian equivalent of a selfie.

The beauty of the thematic approach is that, once you have your themes, you suddenly have a direction and a trajectory, and this makes essay writing a whole lot easier. However, it must also be noted that extracting themes in the first place is something students often find tricky. I have come across many candidates who understand the extract and the novella inside out; but when they are presented with a question under exam conditions, and the pressure kicks in, they find it tough to break their response down into themes. The fact of the matter is: the process is a *creative* one and the best themes require a bit of imagination.

In this guide, I shall take seven different exam-style questions, coupled with extracts from the novella, and put together a plan for each – a plan that illustrates in detail how we will be satisfying the mark scheme's criteria. Please do keep in mind that, when operating under timed conditions, your plans will necessarily be less detailed than those that appear in this volume.

Now, you might be asking whether three or four themes is best. The truth is, you should do whatever you feel most comfortable with: the examiner is looking for an original, creative answer, and not sitting there counting the themes. So if you think you are quick enough to cover four, then great. However, if you would rather do three to make sure you do each theme justice, that's also fine. I sometimes suggest that my student pick four themes, but make the fourth one smaller – sort of like an afterthought, or an observation that turns things on their head. That way, if they feel they won't have time to explore this fourth theme in its own right, they can always give it a quick mention in the conclusion instead.

A London mural of Charles Dickens, surrounded by his fictional characters. Directly above Dickens's head, there is a depiction of Scrooge and his famed door-knocker.

Before I move forward in earnest, I believe it to be worthwhile to run through the four Assessment Objectives the exam board want you to cover in your response – if only to demonstrate how effective the thematic response can be. I would argue that the first Assessment Objective (AO1) – the one that wants candidates to 'read, understand and respond to texts' and which is worth 12 of the total 34 marks up for grabs – will be wholly satisfied by selecting strong themes, then fleshing them out with quotes. Indeed, when it comes to identifying the top-scoring candidates for AO1, the mark scheme explicitly tells examiners to look for a 'critical, exploratory, conceptualised response' that makes 'judicious use of precise references' – the word 'concept' is a synonym of theme, and 'judicious references' simply refers to quotes that appropriately support the theme you've chosen.

The second Assessment Objective (AO2) – which is also responsible for 12 marks – asks students to 'analyse the language, form and structure used by a writer to create meanings and effects, using relevant subject terminology where appropriate.' As noted, you will already be quoting from the novella as you back up your themes, and it is a natural progression to then analyse the language techniques used. In fact, this is far more effective than simply observing language techniques (personification here, alliteration there), because by discussing how the language techniques relate to and shape the theme, you will also be demonstrating how the writer 'create[s] meanings and effects.'

Now, in my experience, language analysis is the most important element of AO2 – perhaps 8 of the 12 marks will go towards language analysis. You will also notice, however, that AO2 asks students to comment on 'form and structure.' Again, the thematic approach has your back – because though simply jamming in a point on form or structure will feel jarring, when you bring these points up while discussing a theme, as a means to further a thematic argument, you will again organically be discussing the way it 'create[s] meanings and effects.'

AO3 requires you to 'show understanding of the relationships between texts and the contexts in which they were written' and is responsible for a more modest 6 marks in total. These are easy enough to weave into a thematic argument; indeed, the theme gives the student a chance to bring up context in a relevant and fitting way. After all, you don't want it to look like you've just shoehorned a contextual factoid into the mix.

Finally, you have AO4 – known also as "spelling and grammar." There are four marks up for grabs here. Truth be told, this guide is not geared towards AO4. My advice? Make sure you are reading plenty of books and articles, because the more you read, the better your spelling and grammar will be. Also, before the exam, perhaps make a list of words you struggle to spell but often find yourself using in essays, and commit them to memory.

The front facade of Dickens's first London home, situated in Fitzrovia.

My hope is that this book, by demonstrating how to tease out themes from an extract, will help you feel more confident in doing so yourself. I believe it is also worth mentioning that the themes I have picked out are by no means definitive. Asked the very same question, someone else may pick out different themes, and write an answer that is just as good (if not better!). Obviously the exam is not likely to be fun – my memory of them is pretty much the exact opposite. But still, this is one of the very few chances that you will get at GCSE level to actually be creative. And to my mind at least, that was always more enjoyable – if *enjoyable* is the right word – than simply demonstrating that I had memorised loads of facts.

ESSAY PLAN ONE

READ THE FOLLOWING EXTRACT FROM STAVE ONE (MARLEY'S GHOST) AND ANSWER THE QUESTION THAT FOLLOWS.

This extract is from the very start of the novella. It not only discusses the deceased Marley, but also introduces the reader to Scrooge.

Marley was dead: to begin with. There is no doubt whatever about that. The register of his burial was signed by the clergyman, the clerk, the undertaker, and the chief mourner. Scrooge signed it: and Scrooge's name was good upon 'Change, for anything he chose to put his hand to. Old Marley was as dead as a door-nail.

Mind! I don't mean to say that I know, of my own knowledge, what there is particularly dead about a door-nail. I might have been inclined, myself, to regard a coffin-nail as the deadest piece of ironmongery in the trade. But the wisdom of our ancestors is in the simile; and my unhallowed hands shall not disturb it, or the Country's done for. You will therefore permit me to repeat, emphatically, that Marley was as dead as a door-nail.

Scrooge knew he was dead? Of course he did. How could it be otherwise? Scrooge and he were partners for I don't know how many years. Scrooge was his sole executor, his sole administrator, his sole assign, his sole residuary legatee, his sole friend, and sole mourner. And even Scrooge was not so dreadfully cut up by the sad event, but that he was an excellent man of business on the very day of the funeral, and solemnised it with an undoubted bargain.

The mention of Marley's funeral brings me back to the point I started from. There is no doubt that Marley was dead. This must be distinctly understood, or nothing wonderful can come of the story I am going to relate. If we were not perfectly convinced that Hamlet's Father died before the play began, there would be nothing more remarkable in his taking a stroll at night, in an easterly wind, upon his own ramparts, than there would be in any other middle-aged gentleman rashly turning out after dark in a breezy spot—say Saint Paul's Churchyard for instance—literally to astonish his son's weak mind.

Starting with this extract, explore how Dickens creates a hopeful tone in *A Christmas Carol*.

Write about:

• how Dickens creates a hopeful tone in this extract.

• how Dickens creates a hopeful tone in the novella as a whole.

Introduction

It's important to keep the introduction short and sweet, but also to ensure it packs a punch – after all, you only have one chance to make a first impression on the examiner. I recommend starting the introduction with a short comment on historical context to score early AO3 marks. I would then suggest that you very quickly summarise the thematic gist of your essay.

"Given that Dickens came of age in a Europe still grappling with the dashed hopes of the French Revolution's failures, it is little surprise that redemption fantasies had an outsized presence in the early Victorian imagination.[1] This extract not only cultivates hope by explicitly suggesting that the death under discussion spawned a positive outcome, but also, implicitly, through the narrator's humour and levity. However, the Gothic imagery and Shakespearian allusion can be seen to threaten the hopeful tone."[2]

Theme/Paragraph One: Although death is a phenomenon often associated with despair, Dickens conjures hope by framing death as a circumstance that opens the door to wonderful possibilities.

- Although this extract takes death – a phenomenon synonymous with hopelessness – as its chief subject matter, the structure of its opening sentence is alive with possibilities: the assertion that 'Marley was dead' might seem definitive, yet it is followed *not* by a conclusive full stop, but by a leading colon and the phrase: 'to begin with.'[3] While this is most obviously rhetorical – the narrator is sign-posting the start of his story – it also contains a secret double meaning: namely, a sly insinuation that, though Marley might have been dead 'to begin with,' the situation may now have changed (and this is of course later borne out with the appearance of Marley's Ghost). [*AO1 for advancing the argument with a judiciously selected quote; AO2 for the close analysis of the language*].

- The extract's final paragraph is even more explicit in linking Marley's death to 'wonderful' possibilities: the narrator asserts that if the reader fails to 'distinctly' understand the fact of Marley's death, 'nothing wonderful can come of the story.' 'Wonderful' possibilities, therefore, are not merely on the cards in spite of death, but are explicitly contingent on death. The notion that the hopelessness of death might lead to hopeful possibilities creates not just a hopeful tone, but a miraculous one. Indeed, given the novella's title, there is a tacit invitation to reflect on how, in the New Testament, the tragedy of Christ's crucifixion led to his miraculous return. [*AO1 for advancing the argument with a judiciously selected quote*].

- *Elsewhere in the novella*: The idea that death might conjure hope is revisited when Scrooge confronts his hypothetical death with the Ghost of Christmas Yet to Come. This encounter directly improves Scrooge's hopes for reformation: as Scrooge himself remarks: 'I will not be the man I must have been but for this intercourse.' [*AO1 for advancing the argument with a judiciously selected quote*].

Theme/Paragraph Two: The tactic of obliquely turning the third person narrative into a first person narrative, plus the narrator's gentle humour, cultivates a tone that inspires hope.

- While the novella seems at first glance to be rendered in the third person, one might observe that the narrator intermittently injects himself into proceedings ('I don't mean to say;' 'I don't know how many'), thereby subtly establishing himself as a first person narrator in a way that builds rapport. Moreover, the narrator's tone is full of levity: there is humour in his parsing of the 'dead as a doornail' idiom, in his playful hyperbole ('the Country's done for'), and the visual image of an old father 'rashly turning out' at night.[4] Finally, the reader can detect a distinct moral compass in the way the narrator ribs Scrooge for his inappropriate bargain-hunting ('[Scrooge] solemnised [Marley's death] with an undoubted bargain'). [*AO1 for advancing the argument with a judiciously selected quote; AO2 for the close analysis of the language*].

- The total effect is to signal to the reader that proceedings are in the hands of a benign storyteller, and thus they have reason to hope for a happy outcome – an effect made all the more convincing by the structural choice of establishing the narrator's persona right at the novella's start (this passage being the novella's opening). [*AO2 for discussing how structure shapes meaning*].

- *Elsewhere in the novella*: The narrator later draws a subtle parallel between himself and the didactic Ghost of Christmas Past: he observes that Scrooge was 'as close to it as I am now to you... standing in the spirit at your elbow.'[5] This further establishes a hopeful tone, since it implies that, in the same way Scrooge is being granted vital redemptive instruction from the ghost, so too is the reader from the narrator. [*AO1 for advancing the argument with a judiciously selected quote*].

Theme/Paragraph Three: Dickens creates a hopeful tone here by subtly implying that the world of the living is receiving instruction from previous generations.

- Although appearing during the lampooning of an idiom, the assertion that 'the wisdom of our ancestors is in the simile' powerfully plants in the reader's mind the idea that the wisdom of the deceased is at hand to light the way for the living.[6] This hopeful notion crops up even more firmly with the invocation of 'Hamlet's father' – an individual who, though deceased, appears as an apparition at the start of Shakespeare's play in order to offer his son guidance and instruction.[7] While, again, this allusion appears during a whimsical passage, it nevertheless communicates the same serious point: that the deceased are watching over the living. [*AO1 for advancing the argument with a judiciously selected quote; AO2 for the close analysis of the language; AO3 for placing the text in literary context*].
- *Elsewhere in the novella*: Of course, this conceit of the deceased intervening kindly in the affairs of the living is later literalised with Scrooge's rendezvous with Marley's Ghost. Furthermore, while, like Hamlet's

father, Marley's Ghost strikes a grisly image, his intervention is explicitly to give Scrooge hope for redemption: as Marley observes, he is there to help Scrooge 'shun the path I tread.'

Theme/Paragraph Four: While Dickens deploys a number of techniques to create a hopeful tone, the litany of Gothic and gloomy tropes in the passage render the hope fragile.

- As the reader moves through this extract, they are confronted with a host of Gothic tropes: not just the sheer fact of Marley's death, but all the apparatus that goes along with it: the funeral, the presence of the 'clergyman' and 'undertaker.' Even as the narrative moves away from the circumstances immediately surrounding Marley's funeral, the Gothic imagery persists with the reference to 'St Paul's Churchyard.' Furthermore, while the invocation of Hamlet's father might imply paternal guidance, it must be noted that not only is the ghost in *Hamlet* treated with trepidation (Horatio claims it 'bodes some strange eruption to our state'), but Shakespeare's play ends in tragedy and bloodshed.[8] Indeed, given the mounting interest in Shakespeare in Victorian England, Dickens's audience would have been acutely aware of this fact. [*AO1 for advancing the argument with a judiciously selected quote; AO3 for placing the text in a literary and historical context*].
- The mere presence in this passage of Scrooge – the excessive misanthrope – represents yet another Gothic trope: he seems to embody hopelessness with his indifference ('not so dreadfully cut up by the sad

event') and ill will.[9] The despair he represents is so potent that, at the end of the novella, the reformed Scrooge is still able to trick Mr Cratchit with a *faux* dressing down. [*AO1 for advancing the argument with a judiciously selected quote*].

Conclusion

We have a meaty essay here, so I'm not interested in introducing further themes in the conclusion. Instead, I shall tie together the thematic discussion, before leaving the examiner with an intriguing parting thought.

"Dickens's novella functions on the understanding that hope is only meaningful – and, indeed, necessary – when adversity exists. As a result, the Gothic and despairing undertones should not be construed as subverting the hopeful tone; rather, they are a necessary foil that give the hopeful tones their *reason d'être*.[10] Therefore, for all the tactics Dickens actively deploys to create a hopeful tone, perhaps the most important mechanism of all is, ironically, the deliberate sowing of a dread that gives the hopeful tone its purpose and potency."

ESSAY PLAN TWO

READ THE FOLLOWING EXTRACT FROM
STAVE ONE (MARLEY'S GHOST) AND
ANSWER THE QUESTION THAT FOLLOWS.

This extract takes place just before Marley's Ghost enters Scrooge's room.

It was a very low fire indeed; nothing on such a bitter night. He was obliged to sit close to it, and brood over it, before he could extract the least sensation of warmth from such a handful of fuel. The fireplace was an old one, built by some Dutch merchant long ago, and paved all round with quaint Dutch tiles, designed to illustrate the Scriptures. There were Cains and Abels, Pharaoh's daughters; Queens of Sheba, Angelic messengers descending through the air on clouds like feather-beds, Abrahams, Belshazzars, Apostles putting off to sea in butter-boats, hundreds of figures to attract his thoughts; and yet that face of Marley, seven years dead, came like the ancient Prophet's rod, and swallowed up the whole. If each smooth tile had been a blank at first, with power to shape some picture on its surface from the disjointed fragments of his thoughts, there would have been a copy of old Marley's head on every one.

"Humbug!" said Scrooge; and walked across the room.

After several turns, he sat down again. As he threw his head back in the chair, his glance happened to rest upon a bell, a disused bell, that hung in the room, and communicated for some purpose now forgotten with a chamber in the highest story of the building. It was with great astonishment, and with a strange, inexplicable dread, that as he looked, he saw this bell begin to swing. It swung so softly in the outset that it scarcely made a sound; but soon it rang out loudly, and so did every bell in the house.

This might have lasted half a minute, or a minute, but it seemed an hour. The bells ceased as they had begun, together. They were succeeded by a clanking noise, deep down below; as if some person were dragging a heavy chain over the casks in the wine-merchant's cellar. Scrooge then remembered to have heard that ghosts in haunted houses were described as dragging chains.

Starting with this extract, explore how far Dickens presents Scrooge as a stubborn individual.

Write about:

• how far Dickens presents Scrooge as stubborn in this extract.

• how far Dickens presents Scrooge as stubborn in the novella as a whole.

Introduction

Again, I shall kick things off with some historical context in a bid to score AO3 marks, though this time I plan to augment the context by invoking a second Dickens novel. I shall then, once again, give a rundown of the themes I intend to cover:

"As Britain rapidly industrialised in the early Nineteenth Century, and inequality became increasingly acute, representations of man's capacity for intransigence and cruelty abounded: for instance, Dickens's *Hard Times* (1854) unflinchingly explores the suffering of the factory worker, Stephen Blackpool, at the hands of his cold, unyielding employer.[1] Scrooge at first seems to embody just such stubborn cruelty: Dickens lays bare Scrooge's intransigence through his lifestyle and the sheer spectacle required to engage his attention. Yet Scrooge's speedy reform suggests he had a capacity for compromise all along."

Theme/Paragraph One: Dickens telegraphs Scrooge's stubborn adherence to an ideology of thrift and avarice through his lifestyle choices.

- In this deeply visual passage, what first catches the reader's eye is the fire. However, if the fire is a spectacle, it is a spectacle of scarcity: not only is it 'a very low fire indeed,' but its insufficiency precipitates the tableau of Scrooge huddling absurdly close to it in order to 'extract the least sensation of warmth from such a handful of fuel.' With this image – which, due to the lengthy sentences, the reader is forced to 'brood over' – Dickens is telegraphing that Scrooge is so obsessed with adhering to an ideology of thrift that he refuses not only to provide adequate fuel for Cratchit in the counting house, but for himself, too. There is particular irony in withholding coal, given its status as the archetypal anti-gift in Christmas lore. [*AO1 for advancing the argument with a judiciously selected quote; AO2 for the close analysis of the language*].

- A more subtle lifestyle choice is also evident in this extract: namely, Scrooge's choice to live alone (the fact this was a choice is later made explicit when, with the Ghost of Christmas Past, Scrooge revisits the moment he stubbornly chose money over his former fiancée). Again, this points to his stubborn adherence to his ideology of thrift: he has been so consumed with wealth-accumulation that he is unable to accommodate a partner.

- *Elsewhere in the novella*: However, while Dickens is subtly telegraphing Scrooge's particular ideological intransigence in this extract, he is more heavy-handed elsewhere: for instance, in Scrooge's initial response to the men soliciting charity earlier in the stave.

Theme/ Paragraph Two: The spectacular and melodramatic nature of Marley's arrival can be construed as a tacit acknowledgement of the sheer stubbornness of his audience – only the over-the-top has a hope of budging Scrooge.

- What is perhaps most striking in the extract is the sense of spectacle and excessive fanfare that heralds Marley's Ghost's arrival. The appearance of Marley's likeness in 'each smooth tile' of the fireplace – an escalation on the lone likeness that had appeared in the door knocker – is a spectacle that symbolically outdoes the various biblical spectacles (ranging from 'Angelic messengers descending' to 'Apostles putting off to sea') that had hitherto adorned the tiles. By listing these biblical spectacles in a single sentence, and including the image of 'Marley's face... swallowing up the whole' in the sentence's final clause, Dickens uses form to suggest that Marley's appearance should be considered both part of the same epic moral canon as the bible, but also the most spectacular incident yet. [*AO1 for advancing the argument with a judiciously selected quote; AO2 for the close analysis of the language and for discussing how form shapes meaning*].

- This spectacle is followed by that of the ringing bells, which starts with the solitary bell swinging on its own volition: 'as he looked, he saw this bell begin to swing.' Although this is primarily an aural spectacle, there crucially appears to be causation between Scrooge's act of looking and the spectacle getting underway: it is only 'as he looked' that the bell 'begin[s] to swing.' This notion that the fanfare is *not* incidental, but directly catering to its audience, tacitly acknowledges the degree of Scrooge's stubbornness: Marley's Ghost understands that nothing short of a tailor-made, hyperbolic spectacle has a hope of swaying Scrooge. [*AO1 for advancing the argument with a judiciously selected quote; AO2 for the close analysis of the language*].

- *Elsewhere in the novella*: Interestingly, the Ghost of Christmas Past also understands the necessity of over-the-top spectacles to penetrate Scrooge's stubbornness. The spirit's recreation of Scrooge at school, while seemingly at first a faithful rendering of a historical event, becomes an over-the-top spectacle when fictional characters such as 'Ali Baba' and 'Valentine' suddenly appear at the window. [*AO1 for advancing the argument with a judiciously selected quote*].

Theme/Paragraph Three: However, for all Scrooge's seeming intransigence, his instant credulity that he may be dealing with a supernatural entity suggests that, while he might like to self-define as stubborn, his mind is in fact able to quickly relent to outlandish possibilities.

- There is much in the novella's initial sequences to suggest that Scrooge takes pride in being, and takes pains to self-define as, stubborn. In response to Marley's likeness colonising the tiles, his knee-jerk reaction is to proclaim 'Humbug' – a word used to connote something deceptive or false, and which also happens to be Scrooge's go-to verbal tic for dismissing anything that seeks to alter his worldview. However, it is telling that Scrooge, though alone, feels the need to articulate the word out loud ('"Humbug!" said Scrooge). Dickens seems to be suggesting that Scrooge's scepticism is already floundering, since he is feeling the need to convince himself. [*AO1 for advancing the argument with a judiciously selected quote; AO2 for the close analysis of the language*].
- A mere two paragraphs later (the structural compactness emphasising the quick deterioration of

Scrooge's scepticism), the reader abruptly finds Scrooge tacitly entertaining the notion he is dealing with a supernatural entity: he 'remembered to have heard that ghosts in haunted houses were described as dragging chains.' His quickness to entertain such a thought suggests that, while he may consider himself stubborn, Scrooge in fact always had the capacity to compromise. [*AO1 for advancing the argument with a judiciously selected quote; AO2 for discussing how structure shapes meaning*].

- *Elsewhere in the novella*: Scrooge's dogmatism continues to yield as the novella progresses – so much so that, by the time the Ghost of Christmas Yet to Come transports him, he is actively seeking to internalise moral instruction. Dickens was an adherent of Mesmerism, a movement that gained traction in the early Nineteenth Century, and which posited that human behaviour could be altered through trance-like manipulation. The intrinsic malleability of man that Mesmerism implies might help understand why Dickens felt comfortable dramatising such a rapid reform in Scrooge. [*AO3 for placing the text in historical context*].

Conclusion

On this occasion, I have one final point I'd like to cover: namely, that Scrooge's stubbornness is reflected in the architecture of his home. Once I've covered that, I shall then invoke *Hard Times* once again – not only to nab any remaining AO3 points going spare, but also to tidily bring the essay full-circle.

"Whereas, when Marley appears, his stubbornness in life is represented by his 'ponderous chain,' it seems that Scrooge's is symbolised by the property he inhabits: the immovable-seeming 'lowering pile of building' in which he lives. However, while Dickens goes to great lengths to convey Scrooge's stubborn dogmatism, his overriding takeaway appears to be that stubbornness can always be exorcised, and the capacity to change lies latent in all, whether it be Scrooge, or the utilitarian Mr Gradgrind of *Hard Times* – yet another stubborn ideologue whose worldview wreaks untold pain, but who, like Scrooge, also abruptly sees the error of his ways."

This is Arthur Rackham's illustration of
Scrooge with Marley's Ghost. Rackham was
a famed illustrator – watch out for more of
his illustrations throughout this guide!

ESSAY PLAN THREE

READ THE FOLLOWING EXTRACT FROM STAVE TWO (THE FIRST OF THE THREE SPIRITS) AND ANSWER THE QUESTION THAT FOLLOWS.

At this point in the novella, the Ghost of Christmas Past has transported Scrooge to the schoolhouse of his youth.

They went, the Ghost and Scrooge, across the hall, to a door at the back of the house. It opened before them, and disclosed a long, bare, melancholy room, made barer still by lines of plain deal forms and desks. At one of these a lonely boy was reading near a feeble fire; and Scrooge sat down upon a form, and wept to see his poor forgotten self as he used to be.

Not a latent echo in the house, not a squeak and scuffle from the mice behind the panelling, not a drip from the half-thawed water-spout in the dull yard behind, not a sigh among the leafless boughs of one despondent poplar, not the idle swinging of an empty store-house door, no, not a clicking in the fire, but fell upon the heart of Scrooge with a softening influence, and gave a freer passage to his tears.

The Spirit touched him on the arm, and pointed to his younger self, intent upon his reading. Suddenly a man, in foreign garments: wonderfully real and distinct to look at: stood outside the window, with an axe stuck in his belt, and leading by the bridle an ass laden with wood.

"Why, it's Ali Baba!" Scrooge exclaimed in ecstasy. "It's dear old honest Ali Baba! Yes, yes, I know! One Christmas time, when yonder solitary child was left here all alone, he *did* come, for the first time, just like that. Poor boy! And Valentine," said Scrooge, "and his wild brother, Orson; there they go! And what's his name, who was put down in his drawers, asleep, at the Gate of Damascus; don't you see him! And the Sultan's Groom turned upside down by the Genii; there he is upon his head! Serve him right. I'm glad of it. What business had *he* to be married to the Princess!"

To hear Scrooge expending all the earnestness of his nature on such subjects, in a most extraordinary voice between laughing and crying; and to see his heightened and excited face; would have been a surprise to his business friends in the city, indeed.

Starting with this extract, explore how Dickens presents memory in *A Christmas Carol*.

Write about:

• **how Dickens presents memory in this extract.**

• **how Dickens presents memory in the novella as a whole.**

Introduction

As ever, I shall kick this essay off by placing the text in historical and literary context, and thus ensure I'm scoring early AO3 marks. Then I shall signpost the thematic discussions I'm hoping to cover in the essay.

"Given the Romantic movement's fascination with the powers of memory – indeed, William Wordsworth in 1799 was philosophising on 'spots of time' from childhood that possess a 'fructifying virtue' – it is little surprise that their Victorian predecessors shared their interest.[1] In *A Christmas Carol* – a novella rendered in the past tense, and thus framed as an account of the narrator's memories – Scrooge's own deeply visual memories are presented not merely as 'fructifying,' but as transformative and revelatory. However, memory is also presented as malleable, and can even be construed in the novella as a metaphor for fiction itself."

Theme/Paragraph One: Dickens presents memories as having the capacity to transform an individual's worldview and emotional state. They do so in no small part by allowing the individual to recapture a previous version of themselves.

- As the Ghost of Christmas Past confronts Scrooge with his lonely younger self on Christmas Day, the capacity of memories to induce powerful emotions is quickly made apparent: Scrooge 'wept to see his poor forgotten self as he used to be.' That Scrooge 'wept' in empathy for his younger self is particularly striking given his profound lack of empathy in the previous stave. The insinuation here is that this childhood memory has quickly been able to bulldoze his callousness. [*AO1 for advancing the argument with a judiciously selected quote; AO2 for the close analysis of the language*].

- The phraseology is also reminiscent of William Blake's 'Introduction' to *Songs of Innocence* (a collection Dickens was intimately familiar with), in which the narrator 'wept to hear' a child's song – thereby reaffirming the link between the revisiting of childhood and transformative emotions. [*AO2 for the close analysis of the language; AO3 for placing the text in literary context*].

- It is significant that the memory allows Scrooge to access a 'forgotten self as he used to be.' The memory is not merely sparking empathy in Scrooge by making the sufferer none other than himself, but is also allowing Scrooge to re-familiarise himself with a version of himself that was less callous, and more capable of empathy. At the close of this extract, the narrator observes that Scrooge's 'excited face' would have 'been a surprise to his business friends.' If this outward transformation seems to hint that memory has successfully allowed Scrooge to reinhabit his prelapsarian 'forgotten' self, this is confirmed more explicitly when Scrooge later revisits Fezziwig's party, and the narrator observes that '[Scrooge's] heart and soul were...with his former self.'[2] [*AO1 for advancing the argument with judiciously selected quotes*].

Theme/ Paragraph Two: This extract presents memories as primarily visual phenomena – the other senses, while at times engaged, very much take a backseat.

- As the narrator sets the scene at the start of this extract, the focus is exclusively on the visual: the eye is directed to 'a long, bare, melancholy room;' it is then invited to focus in on 'a lonely boy... reading near a feeble fire.' Although fires that appear in memory sequences can and do engage other senses in the novella, this opening paragraph focuses exclusively on the visual. Indeed, the structural choice of leading with visuals implicitly communicates its primacy. [*AO1 for advancing the argument with a judiciously selected quote; AO2 for discussing how structure shapes meaning*].

- Curiously, the second paragraph *does* explore the memory's auditory dimensions. However, the narrator's idiosyncratic syntax – that is, the way he enumerates the sounds that did not fail to soften Scrooge's heart – leads to a paragraph-long sentence which, while technically a catalogue of sounds, also threatens to negate them through the repetition of the word 'not:' 'Not a latent echo... not a squeak and scuffle from the mice...not a drip from the half-thawed water-spout.' The fact a man – one who is 'wonderfully real and distinct to look at' – then appears 'outside the window' reaffirms the primacy of sight. The window draws attention to the act of seeing, while the phrase 'distinct to look at' suggests that it is only through being *looked at* that this memory can be properly discerned. [*AO1 for advancing the argument with a judiciously selected quote; AO2 for the close analysis of the language*].

- *Elsewhere in the novella*: However, although in this particular memory the visuals seem to be of utmost importance, this does not always hold true. When Scrooge is forced to revisit his breakup with his one-time fiancée, what commands the most attention is the dialogue.

Theme/Paragraph Three: Dickens, by allowing fictional individuals to cameo in the memory, presents memory as susceptible to alteration and exaggeration.

- It ought to be noted that the individual who appears beyond the window in this sequence is not a real person from Scrooge's past; it is 'dear old honest Ali Baba' – that is, a fictional character from *Arabian Nights*. Indeed, so too are 'Valentine' and 'his wild brother Orson.' It appears as though the Ghost of Christmas Past has taken the characters from the fiction the young Scrooge had been reading ('his younger self, intent upon his reading') and spliced them into the memory. As a result, Dickens is presenting memories not as set in stone, but as malleable phenomena that can be amended and embellished. [*AO1 for advancing the argument with a judiciously selected quote*].
- Furthermore, not only does the spirit alter memories, but he also artificially fuses disparate memories together. When the ghost announces that they shall

'see another Christmas' shortly after this extract, two discrete memories are welded together: Scrooge's 'former self grew larger at the words, and the room became a little darker and more dirty.' Although taking place in the same location, the memories are two distinct events; however, verbs such as 'grew' and 'became' convey how, visually, one memory seamlessly morphed into another, indicating how the spirit is manipulating memories to create an artificial sense of continuity. [*AO1 for advancing the argument with a judiciously selected quote; AO2 for the close analysis of the language*].

- <u>*Elsewhere in the novella*</u>: Shortly after this sequence, the Ghost of Christmas Past shows Scrooge a scene from within the home of his one-time fiancée as she sits with her daughter and surrounded by children. Crucially, is it unclear to whom this memory belongs – which emphasises not only that memories are open to manipulation, but that their provenance can also be unclear, further problematising their fidelity.

Conclusion

"Memories are a crucial ingredient in *A Christmas Carol*, and Dickens presents them as multifaceted phenomena: at once revelatory, malleable and visual. Indeed, there are more dimensions to memories, still. The way fictional characters intrude on this memory, for instance, also invites the reader to consider the extent to which memory can be considered a metaphor for fiction itself. In the same way Scrooge is being asked to engage with and learn from the 'shadows' the spirit conjures, so too are we, 'intent upon [our] reading,' being invited to comb the fiction for didactic instruction."

This illustration (another of Rackham's) depicts the sequence that takes place within Scrooge's former fiancée's home.

ESSAY PLAN FOUR

READ THE FOLLOWING EXTRACT FROM STAVE THREE (THE SECOND OF THE THREE SPIRITS) AND ANSWER THE QUESTION THAT FOLLOWS.

At this point in the novella, the Ghost of Christmas Present has taken Scrooge to look inside the Cratchit household on Christmas Day.

"And how did little Tim behave?" asked Mrs. Cratchit, when she had rallied Bob on his credulity, and Bob had hugged his daughter to his heart's content.

"As good as gold," said Bob, "and better. Somehow he gets thoughtful, sitting by himself so much, and thinks the strangest things you ever heard. He told me, coming home, that he hoped the people saw him in the church, because he was a cripple, and it might be pleasant to them to remember upon Christmas Day, who made lame beggars walk, and blind men see."

Bob's voice was tremulous when he told them this, and trembled more when he said that Tiny Tim was growing strong and hearty.

His active little crutch was heard upon the floor, and back came Tiny Tim before another word was spoken, escorted by his brother and sister to his stool before the fire; and while Bob, turning up his cuffs—as if, poor fellow, they were capable of being made more shabby—compounded some hot mixture in a jug with gin and lemons, and stirred it round and round and put it on the hob to simmer; Master Peter, and the two ubiqui-tous young Cratchits went to fetch the goose, with which they soon returned in high procession.

Such a bustle ensued that you might have thought a goose the rarest of all birds; a feathered phenomenon, to which a black swan was a matter of course—and in truth it was something very like it in that house. Mrs. Cratchit made the gravy (ready beforehand in a little saucepan) hissing hot; Master Peter mashed the potatoes with incredible vigour; Miss Belinda sweetened up the apple-sauce; Martha dusted the hot plates; Bob took Tiny Tim beside him in a tiny corner at the table; the two young Cratchits set chairs for everybody, not forgetting themselves, and mounting guard upon their posts, crammed spoons into their mouths, lest they should shriek for goose before their turn came to be helped.

Starting with this extract, discuss how Dickens creates sympathy for Tiny Tim.

Write about:

• **how Dickens creates sympathy for Tiny Tim in this extract.**

• **how Dickens creates sympathy for Tiny Tim in the novella as a whole.**

Introduction

"By the time *A Christmas Carol* appeared in 1843, there had been a number of literary forerunners that had sought to cultivate sympathy for society's economically deprived: William Blake's 'Holy Thursday' (1794), for instance, observes how 'Babes [are] reduced to misery' in 'a rich and fruitful land.' Like Blake, Dickens solicits sympathy by appealing to Christian values. However, while one might have expected Dickens to depict Tiny Tim as 'reduced to misery,' he garners sympathy by instead focusing on the spectacle of Tiny Tim's infirmity, which he then renders as all the more spectacular through Tiny Tim's unrelenting buoyancy."

Theme/Paragraph One: Dickens deliberately makes a visual spectacle of Tiny Tim's infirmity. The spectacle not only solicits sympathy from characters within the book, but from the reader, too.

- Near the opening of this extract, Cratchit relays how Tiny Tim had explicitly conveyed to him a desire to become a spectacle of infirmity: Cratchit remarks that Tiny Tim had expressed how 'he hoped the people saw him in the church, because he was a cripple.' Dickens here is signposting to the reader his technique: by offering up a visual of an individual who is both impoverished and disabled, he is converting an abstraction into flesh and blood – a tactic that Tiny Tim instinctively understands to be a powerful driver of sympathy. [*AO1 for advancing the argument with a judiciously selected quote*].

- Of course, the spectacle of Tiny Tim's infirmity is not reserved exclusively for those in church; rather, it is also deployed in this extract to pull at Scrooge's – and the reader's – heartstrings, as Tiny Tim reappears in a way that makes the spectacle aural as well as visual: 'His active little crutch was heard upon the floor, and back came Tiny Tim.' The way in which Tiny Tim's crutch is almost given agency through the word 'active,' and is able to establish its presence before Tiny Tim himself – via its sound, and by appearing earlier in the sentence – tacitly places the apparatus that connotes Tiny Tim's disability front and centre. Tiny Tim's sunny disposition in the face of adversity (he exclaims 'Hurrah' as the food arrives shortly after this extract) only emphasises his courage, casting him as all the more deserving of sympathy. [*AO1 for advancing the argument with a judiciously selected quote; AO2 for the close analysis of the language*].

- *Elsewhere in the novella*: Tiny Tim becomes such an outsized spectacle of impoverished hardship that, when Scrooge later travels with the Ghost of Christmas Yet to Come, and witnesses Cratchit and his family in a hypothetical future mourn Tiny Tim's death, it is in fact the heart rending spectacle of his absence that induces sympathy.

Theme/Paragraph Two: The emotions induced in others in response to Tiny Tim functions as a prompt and rubric for the readers to follow.[1]

- That Tiny Tim induces a profound emotional response in Bob Cratchit is made plain in this extract: the narrator observes that 'Bob's voice was tremulous' when he recounted his conversation with Tiny Tim, 'and trembled more when he said that Tiny Tim was growing strong and hearty.' 'Tremulous' conveys a sense that Cratchit's emotions are so acute that it is impacting on the modulation of his voice, while the word itself – made up of an ictus, followed by two unstressed syllables – mimics the wavering modulation.[2] It is striking that Cratchit's voice 'trembled more' when noting that 'Tim was growing strong and hearty:' there is a sense that Tiny Tim's wellbeing is built on foundations so shaky that Cratchit's voice ends up trembling in turn. [*AO1 for advancing the argument with a judiciously selected quote; AO2 for the close analysis of the language*].

- If Cratchit's hopeful yet profoundly nervous manner when speaking about Tiny Tim is a prompt that inspires a sympathy, then the way his brother and sister 'escorted [Tiny Tim] to his stool before the fire' seems to offer a rubric to Scrooge and the reader of how to act on that sympathy: namely, by offering assistance. [*AO1 for advancing the argument with a judiciously selected quote*].

- *Elsewhere in the novella*: Later in the novella, when Scrooge is glimpsing at a hypothetical future, the sympathetic behaviour of Scrooge's nephew towards the Cratchits in light of Tiny Tim's death once again functions as both prompt and rubric. When Scrooge's nephew expresses he is 'heartily sorry,' he is extending his sympathy both to Cratchit and his deceased son in a way that Scrooge and the reader are invited to emulate. When he enquiries 'if [he] can be of service to you in any way,' he is offering a rubric of how to act on that sympathy. [*AO1 for advancing the argument with a judiciously selected quote*].

Theme/Paragraph Three: Dickens invokes Christian morality to inspire a charitable and sympathetic attitude towards Tiny Tim.

- Given that this novella revolves around a festival that commemorates the birth of Christ, it is little surprise that it makes use of Christian morality and dogma to cultivate sympathy for Tiny Tim. Cratchit, when recounting how Tiny Tim desires to be treated as a spectacle, explains Tiny Tim's logic: Tiny Tim hopes 'it might be pleasant to them to remember upon Christmas Day, who made lame beggars walk, and blind men see.' Dickens is deploying the example of Christ – the messianic figure who aided the needy – as a means to induce sympathy for the likes of Tiny Tim: he is encouraging others to learn from Christ's moral teachings and adopt his mindset. [*AO1 for advancing the argument with a judiciously selected quote*].

- *Elsewhere in the novella*: References to Christ and Christianity appear time and again throughout the novella in a bid to foster sympathy not just for Tiny

Tim, but for society's most deprived as a whole. For instance, Marley's Ghost in the opening stave bemoans the fact he never raised his eyes 'to that blessed Star which led the Wise Men to a poor abode,' an allusion which not only invokes Christ, but also, by drawing attention to the lowly circumstances of Christ's birth ('a poor abode'), forces the reader to acknowledge that neglecting to have love and sympathy for the poor is an affront to God himself. [*AO1 for advancing the argument with a judiciously selected quote; AO2 for the close analysis of the language*].

- Dickens, by leaning on Christian morality, seems to be tacitly acknowledging that Christianity was already a powerful driver for charity in Victorian Britain. By the late Nineteenth Century, three in every four voluntary societies were run by Evangelicals. [*AO3 for invoking historical context that illuminates the text*].

Theme/Paragraph Four: In some respects, however, Dickens does not portray Tim as pitiable so much as surrounded by love. By contrast, it is Scrooge – the lonely, dejected misanthrope – who seems more warranting of sympathy.

- Arguably, the overwhelming impression of this extract is not that Tiny Tim ought to be the subject of our sympathy; it is that he is in fact enviably surrounded by love. Cratchit's laudatory description of his behaviour ('As good as gold... and better'), the way Cratchit places him in pride of place beside him ('Bob took Tiny Tim beside him in a tiny corner at the table'), and he way he is clucked over by his siblings ('escorted by his brother and sister') combine to create an impression of a boy who is nothing short of the apple of his family's eye. [*AO1 for advancing the argument with a judiciously selected quote; AO2 for the close analysis of the language*].

- Moreover, while the Cratchits might have been poor, the warmth of the home life – from the high spirits of the 'ubiquitous young Cratchits,' to the all-for-one-and-one-for-all mentality implied by the collective food preparation – further enhances the sense that Tiny Tim's existence is one of familial bliss.

- *Elsewhere in the novella*: By contrast, it might be argued that the isolated Scrooge –'quite alone in the world,' as his ex-fiancée's husband puts it – strikes the truly most pitiable figure in the novella. Indeed, the vignette conjured by the Ghost of Christ Yet to Come – in which Scrooge is laid up alone on his death bed, stripped of all worldly possessions – is a *tour de force* in pathos. Whereas Tiny Tim has a 'ubiquitous' family, Scrooge is utterly alone. [*AO1 for advancing the argument with a judiciously selected quote*].

Conclusion

"Dickens, known for his visual style, deftly makes a spectacle of Tiny Tim's infirmity as a means of soliciting sympathy, while also following up with behavioural prompts from the other Cratchits, as well as from Christian moral coda, in order to establish a rubric of sympathetic compassion for Scrooge and the reader to follow. However, there is ultimately a deep ambivalence in the novella, for although Dickens undoubtedly canvasses for sympathy on Tiny Tim's behalf, his novella simultaneously posits Scrooge – the wealthy yet unloved loner – as truly its most pitiable specimen."

ESSAY PLAN FIVE

At this point in the novella, the third spirit – the Ghost of Christmas Yet to Come – is approaching Scrooge for the first time.

The Phantom slowly, gravely, silently, approached. When it came near him, Scrooge bent down upon his knee; for in the very air through which this Spirit moved it seemed to scatter gloom and mystery.

It was shrouded in a deep black garment, which concealed its head, its face, its form, and left nothing of it visible save one outstretched hand. But for this it would have been difficult to detach its figure from the night, and separate it from the darkness by which it was surrounded.

He felt that it was tall and stately when it came beside him, and that its mysterious presence filled him with a solemn dread. He knew no more, for the Spirit neither spoke nor moved.

"I am in the presence of the Ghost of Christmas Yet To Come?" said Scrooge.

The Spirit answered not, but pointed onward with its hand.

"You are about to show me shadows of the things that have not happened, but will happen in the time before us," Scrooge pursued. "Is that so, Spirit?"

The upper portion of the garment was contracted for an instant in its folds, as if the Spirit had inclined its head. That was the only answer he received.

Although well used to ghostly company by this time, Scrooge feared the silent shape so much that his legs trembled beneath him, and he found that he could hardly stand when he prepared to follow it. The Spirit paused a moment, as observing his condition, and giving him time to recover.

But Scrooge was all the worse for this. It thrilled him with a vague uncertain horror, to know that behind the dusky shroud, there were ghostly eyes intently fixed upon him, while he, though he stretched his own to the utmost, could see nothing but a spectral hand and one great heap of black.

Starting with this extract, discuss how Dickens presents The Ghost of Christmas Yet to Come as a terrifying entity.

Write about:

- **how Dickens presents the Ghost of Christmas Yet to Come in this extract.**

- **how Dickens presents the Ghost of**

Christmas Yet to Come in the rest of the novella.

Introduction

"Given that the flourishing Gothic genre occupied an outsized space in the early Victorian imagination, it is little surprise that Dickens found himself aping some of its animating tropes. The Ghost of Christmas Yet to Come is undoubtedly one of the novella's most archetypal Gothic figures: he is presented as terrifying not only though the visceral emotional response he induces, but also in the way he eludes comprehension. However, it might be asserted that what is truly terrifying is not the spirit, but the bleak future – the one extrapolated from Scrooge's current trajectory – that Scrooge realises he must confront in the spirit's company."

Theme/Paragraph One: By presenting the spirit as a figure that Scrooge is unable to discern – either visually or audibly – Dickens casts him as an unknown quantity. Given that comprehending the spirits and their visions is crucial to Scrooge's salvation, the indiscernibility is terrifying.

- Considering that this is a novella in which visuals are paramount, and Scrooge, cast as voyeur-in-chief, is required to depend on his sense of sight, it is striking that the Ghost of Christmas Yet to Come manifests in a way that eludes Scrooge's power of sight.[1] The narrator asserts that the spirit was 'shrouded in a deep black garment,' but then, after establishing the garments existence, proceeds to obscure this garment by observing that, if it was not for the visible 'outstretched hand,' it would have been difficult to detach its figure from the night, and separate it from the darkness. As the shroud finds itself at risk of being itself 'shrouded' by the night, Scrooge finds his vision confronted by a figure that threatens to render it powerless. [*AO1 for advancing the argument with a judiciously selected quote; AO2 for the close analysis of the language*].

- If the spirit thwarts Scrooge's powers of sight, it also evades his auditory capacity by quite simply refusing to talk: the narrator observes that the 'Spirit answered not,' placing the word 'not' after 'answered' to afford it extra emphasis. The Gothic genre frequently sought to explore humankind's instinctive fear of the unknown. By presenting the spirit as an unknown quantity, as a figure who evades and rebuffs Scrooge's senses, Dickens casts him as terrifying in the vein of the Gothic tradition. [*AO1 for advancing the argument with a judiciously selected quote*].

- *Elsewhere in the novella*: However, even more important is the notion that Scrooge's salvation is at stake. Scrooge well understands that discerning both the spirits and their messages is crucial for his immortal soul: shortly after this scene, for instance, the spirit invites Scrooge to listen-in on conversations in a courtyard, and Scrooge does so with religious care, since he is 'assured that they must have some hidden purpose' that is crucial to divine. The spirit's unintelligibility raises the terrifying prospect that Scrooge will fail in this vital trial of interpretation and thus be left to eternal damnation. [*AO1 for advancing the argument with a judiciously selected quote*].

Theme/Paragraph Two: Dickens conveys the spirit as terrifying through the visceral description of its impact on Scrooge: Scrooge undergoes a rapid physical deterioration and experiences profound psychological trauma.

- That the spirit takes a profound psychological toll on Scrooge is made explicit time and again in the passage: he is first 'filled him with a solemn dread,' then, a matter of lines later, he is 'thrilled... with a vague uncertain horror.' The auditory likeness between 'filled' and 'thrilled' adds emphasis by imparting a sense that Scrooge's trauma is both doubling up and metastasizing – while the lexicon would have been a signal to a contemporary reader that Scrooge was undergoing an archetypally Gothic trauma, since the turn of phrase was fast becoming commonplace for articulating terror in the genre. (A year later, Edgar Allan Poe's narrator in 'The Raven' would talk of curtains that 'Thrilled me – filled me with fantastic terrors never felt before'). [*AO1 for advancing the argument with a judiciously selected quote; AO2 for the close analysis of the language; AO3 for placing the text in historical-literary context*].
- However, the spirit's impact is not confined to the psychological: Scrooge also experiences extreme

physical distress, one that chiefly effects his capacity to move and support himself: 'his legs trembled beneath him, and he found that he could hardly stand when he prepared to follow it.' By implanting a paragraph break after the ghost gives Scrooge 'time to recover,' Dickens, through the use of form, creates a pause that reflects Scrooge's temporary paralysis. [*AO2 for discussing how form shapes meaning*].

- *Elsewhere in the novella*: It ought to be noted that, while Marley's Ghost also appears to be a horrifying spectre, his impact on Scrooge is not one of such undiluted terror. Rather, Scrooge's fear is tempered by a subversive and comical incredulity, one that makes clear that Marley's Ghost ultimately lacks the third spirit's Gothic gravitas.

Theme/Paragraph Three: Dickens presents the third spirit as terrifying insofar as he has the ability to show Scrooge the future – tacit here is the expectation that, given Scrooge's past conduct, his future is likely to be bleak.

- It is striking that front and centre of Scrooge's mind is whether the spirit has the power to reveal the future. Immediately after attempting to clarify the spirit's identity, Scrooge enquires if the spirit is 'about to show... shadows of the things that have not happened, but will happen in the time before us' – in fact, Dickens uses the word 'pursued' to describe Scrooge's style of questioning, thereby conveying his urgency. Implicit in this enquiry, given Scrooge's amoral past and the rebukes he has received from his previous supernatural visitors, is Scrooge's understanding that his future is likely to be a bleak and terrifying affair. As a result, since the spirit has taken on the role of messenger of this bleak future, he becomes, by extension, a terrifying presence. [*AO1 for advancing the argument with a judiciously selected quote; AO2 for the close analysis of the language*].

- *Elsewhere in the novella*: However, it might be argued that it is not the spirit who is truly terrifying, but in fact Scrooge himself, for it is his own past conduct that has sown this bleak future. Scrooge's horror at his past conduct is powerfully conveyed during another of the novella's episodes of acute trauma: when the Ghost of Christmas Past confronts him with the life he gave up by terminating his relationship with his ex-fiancée, Belle.

Theme/Paragraph Four: The spirit is presented as terrifying insofar as his physical appearance seems to heavily allude to medieval depictions of death and, specifically, the Grim Reaper.

- While the spirit may be tough to visually discern, there are various aspects of the spirit's physical appearance that *can* be made out – for instance, it's 'deep black garment, which concealed its head;' the way the garment 'contracted... in its folds;' the solitary 'outstretched hand' – and these seem to allude to potent depictions of death. In particular, these details are reminiscent of the Grim Reaper – a figment of medieval society's collective imagination, who, with his black cloak, scythe, and skeletal extremities, was a kind of human embodiment of the Black Death.

Moreover, the way in which Scrooge 'bent down upon his knee' is also evocative of submitting oneself to divine judgment immediately after death. Therefore, given that death so often figures in the human imagination as the ultimate driver of terror, this synonymity between the spirit and death powerfully casts him as a terrifying entity. [*AO1 for advancing the argument with a judiciously selected quote; AO2 for the close analysis of the language; AO3 for invoking historical context to illuminate the text*].

- *Elsewhere in the novella*: It might be noted that the sense that Dickens intended for this spirit to be understood as an incarnation and harbinger of death seems to be emphatically confirmed by the sequence in which the spirit confronts Scrooge with his own grave. Indeed, this interpretation is further supported by the novella's structure: the ghost is the third of three to appear, and appears as the narrative moves into its final third. [*AO2 for discussing how structure shapes meaning*].

Conclusion

"In Emily Bronte's *Wuthering Heights* (1847), a seemingly disembodied hand grasps Lockwood's hand as he reaches through a window, and, in terror, Lockwood scrapes the ghostly hand against shattered glass. The trope of the quasi-disembodied hand appears, too, in *A Christmas Carol* – yet another technique Dickens uses to cast his third spirit as a terrifying entity. However, while Dickens deploys a number of tactics to present the Ghost of Christmas

Yet to Come as terrifying, one cannot escape the fact that its most potent means of inspiring horror – that is, by revealing a bleak future – in fact suggests that the skeletons in Scrooge's closet are truly the novella's most terrifying entity; after all, the future's horrors are entirely a product of Scrooge's past."

A drawing from an early Twentieth Century children's book, depicting Scrooge in the company of the Ghost of Christmas Yet to Come.

ESSAY PLAN SIX

At this point in the novella, the Ghost of Christmas Yet to Come is showing Scrooge an episode in which various individuals who had attended to Scrooge (the laundress, the undertaker, the charwoman) are selling objects they stole from Scrooge's home after his death.

"You couldn't have met in a better place," said old Joe, removing his pipe from his mouth. "Come into the parlour. You were made free of it long ago, you know; and the other two an't strangers. Stop till I shut the door of the shop. Ah! How it skreeks! There an't such a rusty bit of metal in the place as its own hinges, I believe; and I'm sure there's no such old bones here, as mine. Ha, ha! We're all suitable to our calling, we're well matched. Come into the parlour. Come into the parlour."

The parlour was the space behind the screen of rags. The old man raked the fire together with an old stair-rod, and having trimmed his smoky lamp (for it was night), with the stem of his pipe, put it in his mouth again.

While he did this, the woman who had already spoken threw her bundle on the floor, and sat down in a flaunting manner on a stool; crossing her elbows on her knees, and looking with a bold defiance at the other two.

"What odds then! What odds, Mrs. Dilber?" said the woman. "Every person has a right to take care of themselves. He always did."

"That's true, indeed!" said the laundress. "No man more so."

"Why then, don't stand staring as if you was afraid, woman; who's the wiser? We're not going to pick holes in each other's coats, I suppose?"

"No, indeed!" said Mrs. Dilber and the man together. "We should hope not."

"Very well, then!" cried the woman. "That's enough. Who's the worse for the loss of a few things like these? Not a dead man, I suppose."

"No, indeed," said Mrs. Dilber, laughing.

"If he wanted to keep 'em after he was dead, a wicked old screw," pursued the woman, "why wasn't he natural in his life-time? If he had been, he'd have had somebody to look after him when he was struck with Death, instead of lying gasping out his last there, alone by himself."

Starting with this extract, discuss how

Dickens makes use of strangers in *A Christmas Carol.*

Write about:

• how Dickens makes use of strangers in this extract.

• how Dickens makes use of strangers in the novella as a whole.

Introduction

"Considering that London during the early Nineteenth Century experienced a population explosion – so much so that, by 1851, it played host to over 27 million – it is little wonder that a fascination with strangers permeated artistic portrayals of the city. By hop-scotching through the lives of those Scrooge refers to as 'surplus population,' Dickens's novella not only gives insight into the lives of the economically deprived, but is also able to conjure a series of vignettes (such as in this extract) that complement his episodic technique. It might also be noted that Dickens depicts the isolated Scrooge as striving to relegate the entirety of mankind to the status of stranger."

Theme/Paragraph One: In this extract, the conversation between the strangers is used to illustrate how Scrooge has relegated the entirety of mankind to the status of stranger.

- Near the close of this extract – which takes places in a hypothetical future, shortly after Scrooge's death – the unnamed woman observes that if Scrooge had been 'natural in his lifetime,' then 'he'd have had somebody to look after him when struck with Death,' as opposed to winding up 'by himself.' Dickens is thus using a stranger to spell out Scrooge's pathological and un-'natural' habit of treating the entirety of mankind as a collection of strangers. Indeed, her comment is emphatically confirmed by the sheer fact that, although she worked as a domestic for Scrooge while he was alive, he does not recognise her: not only does she go unnamed in the narrative ('said the woman;' 'cried the woman'), but also, after this sequence, Scrooge absurdly fails to realise that *he* is her 'wicked old screw' of an employer. [*AO1 for advancing the argument with a judiciously selected quote; AO2 for the close analysis of the language*].
- <u>Elsewhere in the novella</u>: In a sense, at least from the pre-reformed Scrooge's point of view, the novella's entire *dramatis personae* are to be seen as strangers, since he wishes to sever himself from all human interactions beyond those strictly predicated in business. Indeed, this can be seen in his dismissive treatment of his nephew in the opening stave; in his desire to be rid of Marley's Ghost; and in the way his various business acquaintances are forever unnamed. Therefore, Dickens uses the mere presence of characters Scrooge has pushed away – and who can thus be considered pseudo-strangers, regardless of whether Scrooge might technically know their identity – as a means to illustrate Scrooge's pathological effort to estrange himself from society.

Theme/Paragraph Two: Dickens uses the cruelty of the strangers in this extract to subtly show how Scrooge's own cruelty has been internalised by those who have entered his orbit.

- One of the most striking aspects of this passage is the callousness of the strangers' behaviour. Their very mission is a cruel one: the three visitors are preparing to sell the items they have plundered from Scrooge to Old Joe. However, their callous attitude towards the deceased is exemplified by the unnamed woman, who leans on a cold utilitarianism to excuse their theft: 'Who's the worse for the loss of a few things like these? Not a dead man.' [*AO1 for advancing the argument with a judiciously selected quote*].

- However, the callousness is not limited to the unnamed woman. Old Joe is monstrously unempathetic with his blasé jokes – 'I'm sure there's no such old bones here, as mine. Ha, ha!' – and takes pleasure in the turn of events: 'You couldn't have met in a better place.' Not only do Old Joe's comments, by appearing at the start of the vignette, structurally set the tone for the sequence, but the callous use of 'better place' is also deeply ironic, given its more conventional use as a respectful euphemism for the afterlife. That Mrs Dilber is seen 'laughing' at the unnamed woman's attempt to rationalise their behaviour illustrates the contagiousness of this toxic humour. [*AO1 for advancing the argument with a judiciously selected quote; AO2 for the close analysis of the language and for discussing how structure shapes meaning*].

- The implication in this passage is that these strangers'

callousness is a direct result of Scrooge's cruelty: indeed, the unnamed woman all but draws a direct link: 'Every person has a right to take care of themselves. He always did.' *Elsewhere in the novella*: However, while this passage implies that cruelty begets cruelty, Dickens uses other strangers to illustrate that this is not always the case. The Cratchits – all of whom (bar Bob) are strangers to Scrooge – continue functioning with kindness and warmth, despite Scrooge's malign influence in their lives. [*AO1 for advancing the argument with a judiciously selected quote*].

Theme/Paragraph Three: Although the characters in this extract exhibit cruelty, they also exhibit desperation. As a result, this sequence represents one of many instances in which Dickens uses strangers to explore the hardships of the economically deprived.

- While the unnamed woman's assertion that 'every person has a right to take care of themselves' can be construed as a rationalisation of cruelty, this mentality can equally be seen quite simply as a necessary evil for the most economically deprived in society. Indeed, the sense that these individuals are going to these lengths *not* out of greed, but ultimately out of necessity, is hinted at through the unnamed woman's body language: namely, the way she 'look[s] with a bold defiance at the other two.' The word 'bold' almost suggests courage, while 'defiance' has resonances of moral credence and self-righteousness.

[AO1 for advancing the argument with a judiciously selected quote; AO2 for the close analysis of the language].

- <u>*Elsewhere in the novella*</u>: Dickens uses strangers throughout the book as a means to explore the suffering and extremes that characterise the daily lives of the poorest in society – whether it be the carol singer at Scrooge's door in the opening stave, Tiny Tim, or the couple who, in the hypothetical future, find themselves guiltily rejoicing in Scrooge's death, since it releases them from their debt to him. The struggling poor Dickens represents reflect the realities of Victorian London, which was not only heavily populated, but also plagued with economic deprivation, with some 30,000 homeless children living on London's streets by 1848. [*AO3 for providing insight through relevant historical context*].

Theme/Paragraph Four: Dickens uses strangers to complement and better achieve the episodic style *A Christmas Carol* strives to embody.

- Dickens's novella, revolving as it does around the whistle-stop tours conducted by three supernatural guides, is deeply episodic in nature, and Dickens uses strangers as a means of generating fodder for these episodes. This sequence with Old Joe is characterised by the same techniques Dickens uses throughout the novella to lend sequences an episodic feel. Old Joe's verbal and aesthetic idiosyncrasies – ranging from his fondness of the contracted 'an't' to the 'pipe' in his mouth – are established quickly, and so too is the 'parlour.'[1] Together, these details anchor the scene, giving the spectator – be it Scrooge or the reader – instant focal points. Moreover, by observing how Joe 'raked the fire together with an old stair-rod,' Dickens quickly establishes a highly visual tableau, one that subtly connects it to the novella's other tableaux involving fireplaces. [*AO*1 *for advancing the argument with a judiciously selected quote; AO*2 *for the close analysis of the language*].

- Elsewhere in the novella: Throughout the novella, Dickens makes use of strangers as fodder for his episodic spectacles, such as when the Ghost of Christmas Present shows Scrooge a quickly-resolved fight between two men, or leads Scrooge around a ship out at sea. However, strangers do not just provide fodder for these episodes; they also reflect the variety these episodes imply. If an episodic novella seeks to tell a multitude of short tales, a multitude of strangers implicitly embodies a multitude of tales.

Conclusion

"At one point in Stave Two, Scrooge looks at the first spirit's face and observes that 'in some strange way there were fragments of all the faces it had shown him.' With this, Dickens reminds us that the spirits, too, are strangers – in fact, the first seems to embody *all* strangers – and that their didactic function represents yet another role strangers play in the text. Indeed, the didactic power of these supernatural strangers is so profound that Scrooge ends up utterly changed; so much so that Cratchit, who 'an't [a] stranger' to

Scrooge's counting-house, finds himself confronted in
the novella's finale by a totally different Scrooge: a
stranger to the one he once knew."

This is an illustration from Arthur Rackham -
this time, his take on the incident that
unfolds in the extract above.

ESSAY PLAN SEVEN

In this extract, which appears at the end of the novella, a reformed Scrooge plays a practical joke on Bob Cratchit.

The clock struck nine. No Bob. A quarter past. No Bob. He was full eighteen minutes and a half behind his time. Scrooge sat with his door wide open, that he might see him come into the Tank.

His hat was off, before he opened the door; his comforter too. He was on his stool in a jiffy; driving away with his pen, as if he were trying to overtake nine o'clock.

"Hallo!" growled Scrooge, in his accustomed voice, as near as he could feign it. "What do you mean by coming here at this time of day?"

"I am very sorry, sir," said Bob. "I *am* behind my time."

"You are?" repeated Scrooge. "Yes. I think you are. Step this way, sir, if you please."

"It's only once a year, sir," pleaded Bob, appearing from the Tank. "It shall not be repeated. I was making rather merry yesterday, sir."

"Now, I'll tell you what, my friend," said Scrooge, "I am not going to stand this sort of thing any longer. And therefore," he continued, leaping from his stool, and giving Bob such a dig in the waistcoat that he staggered back into the Tank again; "and therefore I am about to raise your salary!"

Bob trembled, and got a little nearer to the ruler. He had a momentary idea of knocking Scrooge down with it, holding him, and calling to the people in the court for help and a strait-waistcoat.

"A merry Christmas, Bob!" said Scrooge, with an earnestness that could not be mistaken, as he clapped him on the back. "A merrier Christmas, Bob, my good fellow, than I have given you, for many a year! I'll raise your salary, and endeavour to assist your struggling family, and we will discuss your affairs this very afternoon, over a Christmas bowl of smoking bishop, Bob! Make up the fires, and buy another coal-scuttle before you dot another i, Bob Cratchit!"

Starting with this passage, discuss how Dickens presents deception in *A Christmas Carol*.

Write about:

- **how Dickens presents deception in this extract.**

- **how Dickens presents deception in the novella as a whole.**

Introduction

'Given that Dickens cut his teeth writing plays as opposed to novels – his first play, *The Strange Gentleman* (1836), was performed some sixty times – it is perhaps unsurprising that when the theme of deception arises in his novels/novellas, it often figures as something deeply theatrical. In this extract, the reformed Scrooge puts on a performance for Cratchit by affecting an animus he no longer feels. However, if Dickens presents deception as theatrical, and, indeed, as a tool used to build rapport, he also, by exploring Cratchit's raw reaction, portrays deception as a catalyst of powerful emotions.'

Theme/Paragraph One: Performance and spectacle are presented in this extract not merely as a means of achieving deception, but as an intrinsic part of deception.

- There is a profound sense that Scrooge, as he plays his practical joke, is putting on a performance. For starters, there is an initial sense that he is something akin to an actor waiting in the wings: the way in which the narrator's free and indirect style implies that Scrooge is counting the minutes till Cratchit arrives – 'The clock struck nine. No Bob. A quarter past. No Bob.' – subtly casts him as an actor waiting for his cue, while the space up to and including 'the Tank' feels almost as if a stage he is waiting to tread.[1] [*AO1 for advancing the argument with a judiciously selected quote; AO2 for the close analysis of the language*].

- Once Cratchit arrives, and Scrooge's prank gets underway, the sense of it being a performance becomes all the more pronounced: the narrator observes that Scrooge talks in 'his accustomed voice, as near as he could feign it.' Scrooge is not merely speaking the lines, but is carefully adjusting his tone to affect a persona: the phrase 'near as he could' indicates an effort to calibrate his tone against a benchmark, and underscores it as a performance. Moreover, the quick-fire dialogue, creating a litany of short paragraphs, causes the mise-en-page to subtly reflect a play-script.[2] [*AO1 for advancing the argument with a judiciously selected quote; AO2 for the close analysis of the language and for discussing how form shapes meaning*].

- *Elsewhere in the novella*: When, in Stave Two, the Ghost of Christmas Past transports Scrooge back to school, Scrooge observes how fictional characters from the book his younger self is reading can be seen outside the window. The reader understands that these fictional individuals never truly existed in Scrooge's past, and thus that their presence is a deception. When combined with the fact they appear beyond a window frame – a frame which tacitly casts their presence as a performance and a spectacle – the link between deception and performance becomes all the more profound.

Theme/Paragraph Two: The art of practical joking – a specific type of deception – is presented in this passage as something intended to be light-hearted and jocular, and that stems from a desire to build rapport.

- Scrooge's whole objective here is to play a practical joke: that is, to temporarily affect ill-will towards Cratchit. Naturally enough, the jocularity only reveals itself once Scrooge wishes to cease his deception (it would, after all, give the game away if it appeared any sooner) and manifests in the first instance with Scrooge's body language: namely, his 'giving Bob such a dig in the waistcoat.' The sheer boyish exuberance of the action – it is not just a dig, but 'such a dig' – expresses Scrooge's hunger to build rapport that motivated the deception in the first place. [*AO1 for advancing the argument with a judiciously selected quote; AO2 for the close analysis of the language*].

- That Scrooge intends for Cratchit to see his act of deception as a good natured joke is further confirmed by the fact he follows up with well wishes (which he extends 'with an earnestness that could not be mistaken'), and yet more body language: 'he clapped [Cratchit] on the back.' Not only is this an intimate gesture in itself, but it is also a seems to hint at the idiom *to pat on the back*, thus telegraphing appreciation and admiration. [*AO1 for advancing the argument with a judiciously selected quote; AO2 for the close analysis of the language*].

- Elsewhere in the novella: Dickens presents practical jokes as a well-meaning effort to build rapport earlier in the novella, too – specifically, when Martha hides at the Cratchits' house just before Bob Cratchit arrives, and deceiving him into momentary disappointment. The symmetry between these two incidents subtly seems to suggest that, with his practical joke, Scrooge has begun to behave as though a member of Cratchit's family.

Theme/Paragraph Three: In this extract, Dickens presents deception as something that can induce strong emotions in the individual being deceived – emotions that are not altogether positive.

- In Stave Three, Martha brings her practical joke on Cratchit to a premature close, the narrator informs the reader, because she 'didn't like to see him disappointed, if it were only in joke.' With this observation, Dickens spells out another dimension of deception: that even when carried out with the best intentions, it can still induce strong negative emotions. Indeed, this is precisely the case in this extract. As Scrooge's play-acting reaches its denouement, and he combines a sudden 'dig in the waistcoat' with the disorientating announcement that he intends to 'raise [Cratchit's] salary,' Cratchit's reaction is a fight-or-flight anxiety.[3] The narrator observes how Bob 'trembled' – the trochaic word mirroring his wavering state – and how he even entertains the idea of violence: he considers 'knocking Scrooge down with [a ruler], holding him, and calling to the people in the court for help and a strait-waistcoat.'⁴ [*AO1 for advancing the argument with a judiciously selected quote; AO2 for the close analysis of the language*].

- *Elsewhere in the novella*: However, in *A Christmas Carol*, it is not only deception that can induce strong negative emotions: the threat of deception can do so, too. In the opening stave, the reader sees that Scrooge construes Christmas as a kind of financial deception – something that depletes his resources by 'picking [his] pocket every twenty-fifth of December' – and it is this conviction of a grand deception that seems to induce such vitriol in Scrooge. [*AO1 for advancing the argument with a judiciously selected quote*].

Conclusion

"Perhaps the most significant facet to deception in *A Christmas Carol* is in fact its didactic function: the way in which deception is used to educate and reform. This is best exemplified by the Ghost of Christmas Yet to Come, given that, in a sense, everything this didactic ghost shows Scrooge is a deception, since it is all merely hypothetical. Moreover, while deception's moral powers are not obviously on show in this particular extract, the end-product of its didacticism is embodied in the reformed Scrooge, filled as he is with newfound good cheer: 'A merry Christmas Bob.'"

Once again, Arthur Rackham has us covered! This is his take on this practical joke sequence at the end of the novella, with Scrooge (on the right) taking Cratchit by surprise.

NOTES

ESSAY PLAN ONE

1. The 1789 French Revolution was originally an effort to overthrow the aristocracy and create a more equitable society. However, this was quickly followed by The Reign of Terror, in which, under the auspices of Maximilien Robespierre (the revolutionary who seized power), there were brutal public massacres.
2. An allusion is when a writer references something – for instance, a different work of literature or a work of art.
3. You might know that the word synonym is used to describe a word that has a similar meaning to another word: for instance, 'content' is a synonym of 'happy'. However, in this sentence, I'm using the word 'synonymous' to point out how one concept is intimately linked with another.
4. Hyperbole is another word for exaggeration.
5. To be didactic is to be morally instructive.
6. To lampoon something is to mock it.
7. In *Hamlet*, the eponymous main character is tasked with avenging his dead father, the previous king, who was murdered and usurped by Hamlet's uncle, Claudius. Since, at the start of the play, Hamlet's father is already dead, he has no choice but to appear in ghost-form to relay his message!
8. Horatio is Hamlet's closest friend in the play.
9. Misanthropy is the hatred of all people.
10. Reason d'être is a French term. Something's reason d'être is its reason to exist.

ESSAY PLAN TWO

1. Stephen Blackpool's employer, Mr Bounderby, presents himself throughout the novel as a self-made man who, from a hard start in life, has risen to the status of successful businessman. However, it ultimately turns out that he is a fraud, and that he in fact had plenty of privilege in his younger years.

ESSAY PLAN THREE

1. William Wordsworth was one of the most important poets in the Romantic movement, and this meditation on 'spots of time' is from his autobiographical poem, *The Prelude*. The word 'fructifying' means to make something fruitful; so, in other words, he is saying memories possess a particularly useful and productive kind of virtue.
2. Prelapsarian refers to the state of Adam and Eve (in the Old Testament) before they were exiled from Eden. However, it can be used more generally to refer to someone's state prior to a lapse of some kind.

ESSAY PLAN FOUR

1. A rubric is a bit like a template. It's a set of guidelines and rules that are put in place for people to follow.
2. An ictus is a word used to describe stressed syllables. In the word 'trembling,' the first syllable is stressed, whereas the next two are not. To illustrate further, the name 'Dickens' is made up of an ictus followed by one unstressed syllable.

ESSAY PLAN FIVE

1. A voyeur is someone who watches the activities of others.

ESSAY PLAN SIX

1. A person's idiosyncrasies are kind of like their unique character traits.

ESSAY PLAN SEVEN

1. The phrase 'waiting in the wings' is used to describe actors who are waiting in the hidden areas just next to the stage (known as the wings) in preparation for their turn to enter the stage.
   When I talk about the narrator's free and indirect style, I am referring to the way in which the narrator recounts events in the third person, and yet sometimes seems to be inside Scrooge's head, almost as if he has direct access to Scrooge's thoughts. We are not being given unmediated first-person access to Scrooge's thoughts, but with the free and indirect we are being given the next best thing.

2. The mise-en-page – a French expression – refers to the way the text appears on the page.
3. Denouement is a French word that has entered into English usage and refers to the climax of a narrative.
4. A trochaic word is a word that contains two syllables – the first of which is stressed, and the second of which is unstressed. The name 'Cratchit,' for instance, is trochaic, since we put the emphasis on 'Crat' as opposed to 'chit.'

An iambic word also has two syllables – but, contrary to a trochaic word, it has the stress on the second syllable, and not on the first. A name like 'Marie,' for example, is iambic.